# Water Fights

# Water Fights

*What's the Problem?*

Launa Ellison

**To order additional copies of this book, contact:**
Xlibris Corporation
1-888-795-4274
www.Xlibris.com
Orders@Xlibris.com
81806

# CONTENTS

# Chapter 1

# THE BEGINNINGS

*The wars of this century were fought over oil.*
*The wars of the next century will be about water.*

—Ismail Serageldin, World Bank vice president


*Today's real borders are not between nations,*
*But between the powerful and the powerless,*
*free and fettered, privileged and humanitarian.*
*Today, no walls can separate humanitarian or human*
*rights crises in one part of the world from national security*
*crisis in another.*

—Kofi Annan, Nobel Peace Prize acceptance speech,
December 2001

Ever had a water fight? Was it fun? Did you enjoy it? You won't enjoy this one. In 2007, many countries began to fight with one another over water. Water fights, since then, have become more and more common. The Sierra Club stated, "In 2000, 508 million people lived in thirty-one water stressed/scarce countries. By 2025, 3 billion people will live in such places. Today, 20% of the global population lacks access to safe drinking water while 50% live without adequate water sanitation." Over four thousand children worldwide die each day by drinking polluted water. What does "water sanitation" mean to you?

In the United States, we use more than 400 billion gallons of water a day. Northern Kenya uses about 2 billion gallons a day. The Indian Coke company has plants that use 500,000 gallons a day to make soft drinks, and they pour out the residue sludge containing large amounts of lead and cadmium that destroy cropland. In Nigeria, fishermen have taken the Coke company to their high court, seeking to block the release of toxic waste that is polluting their rivers.

Sidebar: What do you already know about water issues? Start a water journal. Date the first page, and write down everything you already know about water issues. Decorate the front cover. Now estimate how much water your home uses each day. Here are the categories to think about: drinking, cooking, brushing your teeth, washing your hands, taking showers and baths, flushing the toilet, watering plants indoors, and watering the yard in the summer.

Does your family buy bottled water? Survey your class and find out how many families buy water. Enter the information in your water journal.

The demand for bottled water is increasing worldwide. However, in the United States, the demand is slowing. It is expected to grow only 6.7% in the next year. Some cities, such as San Francisco, Salt Lake City, and Minneapolis, have banned the use of city monies for bottled water. The United Arab Emirates is the number 1 user of bottled water, with Mexico and Italy tied for second place. France and China export the most water, while the United States, Hong Kong, and Japan are the biggest importers.

Aquafina bottled water comes directly from taps in Detroit and San Francisco. The Dasani brand is also filtered tap water. The Natural Resources Defense Council (NRDC) estimates 40% of bottled water is simply tap water. Ice Mountain pumps more than half a million gallons of tap water each day to make bottles. For a $100 license and millions of dollars of tax credits, it drains public water. Why are these companies allowed to make big money from your city's tap water? Does bottled water taste better? Not according to the results of ABC's *20/20* TV show, in which people could not tell the difference between bottled and tap water. The Evian brand, which is the most expensive, scored the lowest. You're paying ten thousand times as much for bottled water than for tap water. Tap water costs your family about 1 cent per gallon, depending on the region. Tap water is constantly tested. The NRDC has found unwanted chemicals in one-third of the one thousand bottles of water it tested. Worldwide, $100 billion is spent on bottled water. The United Nations' goal of providing everyone with drinkable water by 2015 would only cost $11.3 billion. Make a graph of both billions to better understand the difference.

The price of bottled water includes the cost of oil needed to create the plastic bottles and the cost of transportation. In San Francisco, you can buy water from Fiji (5,455 miles away) and Norway (5,194 miles away). That amounts to a huge distance. In one year, more than 47 million gallons of oil are used to make plastic water bottles. Americans throw away over 30 million plastic water bottles every day. Ninety percent of these bottles are not recycled. A bottle may take one thousand years to decompose and, in the process, may be harming our future water supply. The Blu company in Great Britain makes plastic bottles out of corn; these bottles decompose in only twelve years.

**What are the other water concerns in the United States?**

Let's start with droughts. There are often extreme droughts in Southern California and western Arizona. As part of the droughts,

California has had massive forest fires that have displaced over half a million people. The president has declared the situation in Southern California a national disaster. North Dakota and Northern Minnesota often have droughts. Lake Superior has lost two feet of water, causing shipping problems and changes in the surrounding ecology. Birmingham, Alabama, recently spent $2.4 million looking for new water sources.

Atlanta has watering restrictions. No watering outside homes is allowed except for personal food gardens and newly installed landscapes, and that too only for thirty days. Golf courses are allowed a limited amount of water. Sod producers, food and fiber businesses, retail garden centers, and construction sites have no restrictions. Lake Lanier in northern Georgia is the main source of water for most people in Alabama, Florida, and Georgia, as well as the three million in Atlanta. On October 24, 2007, Lake Lanier's water level was down by fifteen feet. This was the worst drought in the last one hundred years, with the rainfall 50% less than the previous year. Corn, soybean, and peanut crops have failed to survive. Many species of aquatic life are endangered.

**What are your water needs?**

Each and every cell in your body must have water. Babies' bodies are close to 90% water, and adults' bodies are over half water. People who do not take enough water experience heartburn, gastritis, ulcers, hiatal hernias, heart/angina pain, high blood pressure, headaches, rheumatoid joint pains, back pain, and leg pain. Older people lose their sense of thirst and often become dehydrated. Do your grandparents have any of these symptoms? Researchers believe there is a link between dehydration and Alzheimer's. Lack of water causes stress, and stress causes further dehydration.

Now that you have written your reflection about your family's use of water, here is the basic information. An average bath takes 40 gallons of water, and a shower about 5 gallons a minute. If you leave the tap on when you brush your teeth, you are using 4-6 gallons. One toilet flush uses between 3-6 gallons. Low water toilets are required in new buildings. Washing clothes uses 20-30 gallons, and the dishwasher uses 15-20 gallons. The average American drinks 2.5 liters a day—a healthy plan is at least eight glasses a day. In the United States, a family of four will use 250 gallons of water a day. The average rural African family uses about 5 gallons a day.

Web sites:

www.drought.uni.edu/dm/monitor.htlm
www.atlantawatersher.org
www.watercure.com

www.wmrmag.com/stories/jun07/compact.htm

www.umn.edu/outreach/index.html

www.stopcorporateabuse.org

http://ga.water.usgs.gov/edu

Books:

*Troubled Water* by Anita Roddick

*Water Consciousness* edited by Tara Lohan

# CHAPTER 2

# AGRICULTURAL ISSUES

*Throughout the history of literature, the guy who*
*poisons the well has been the worst of all villains.*

—Anonymous

*When the wells dry we know the worth of water.*

—Benjamin Franklin

Agriculture uses about 70% of our water, and industries use 22%. How much does that leave for household needs? It takes 74 gallons of water to create one cup of coffee and over 750 gallons to make a fast food meal of a hamburger and french fries. Raising beef takes ten times as much water as raising peanuts, a similar protein. It takes 18.5 gallons to grow an apple and 36 gallons for one egg. It takes over 700 gallons of water to make a cotton T-shirt. Imagine how much it takes to create a car!

Water pollution is another major issue. In 2003, Jami Harper of Grand Island, Nebraska, discovered that her family and others in the same locality had been using dangerously polluted water for years. The chemicals in their water could cause damage in the liver, lungs, and nervous system and even lead to cancer. These families eventually had to use bottled water for everything, including bathing. Now an architectural engineering major, Jami takes her water road show into elementary classrooms.

In Pennsylvania, corporate feedlots were polluting the water. A program, "Defending Water for Life," attracted public attention to this, and eventually, the Community Environmental Legal Defense Fund was created, and ordinances were passed. Many communities now have similar laws.

A new challenge is posed by ethanol plants. Ethanol is supposed to help us with oil dependency, and the Cargill company went about building a plant in southern Minnesota, intending to produce 100 million gallons of ethanol each year. That would mean many jobs for the region. Unfortunately, the plant would need 350 million gallons of water a year, which was not available. It takes 4 gallons of water to create a gallon of ethanol. Farmers in the area needed the water for irrigation and their livestock. Farm pesticides had also polluted the groundwater. Cargill is one of three companies that applied for water permits and were turned down by the hydrogeologists at the Minnesota Department of Natural Resources (DNR).

Urban sprawl is eating up our most fertile farmland at a rate 30% faster than that of less-productive farming areas. Texas paved over 333,000 acres of farmland in five years. Ohio, Georgia, and North Carolina each lost about 200,000 acres. More than 85% of our fruits and vegetables are grown near cities, and the freshness suffers because of the urban sprawl.

# CHAPTER 3

# WATER ECOSYSTEMS

*The cycle of life is intricately tied up with the*
*cycle of water.*

—Jacques Cousteau


*Water is the blue soul of the planet.*

—Pedro Arrojo Auda


What happens to wildlife when our lakes and rivers are polluted? What happens when our marshes are drained for urban sprawl? What happens to the balance of nature in our earth's ecosystem?

What has happened so far? The January 2003 report in *World-Watch* provided the following information. One-fifth of all freshwater fish are threatened or already extinct apart from 67% of the world's mussels (clams), 51% of the crayfish, and 40% of the amphibians. More than one thousand bird species depending on water for food are threatened. The United States has lost 50% of its wetlands, also know as marshes. Their combined area is greater than that of California, Nevada, and Oregon combined. Both Germany and France have lost 80% of their wetlands, while California has lost 90%. Do some research about marshes, then write a story about an experience in a marsh. You may be yourself or an animal.

In Mexico's Sonoran Desert, agriculture has used 97% of the water. As a result, the migratory bird population has dropped by more than half. Today, fewer than a hundred thousand birds come to this area. Beluga whales in the St. Lawrence Seaway have dangerously high levels of PCBs in their blubbers as a result of water pollution.

There are twenty-five designated biodiversity "hot spots," including Mexico, Central America, the Caribbean, the western United States, the Mediterranean Basin, southern Africa, and southwestern China. In some areas, the "point of no return" is believed to have been reached.

China has 22% of the world's population. Its rivers are running dry, and ancient aquifers will take thousands of years to regenerate. Its formerly magnificent rivers are now sluggish with pollution, and wildlife has almost disappeared. China's three productive fisheries have dropped by half, eliminating jobs. There are about a hundred rare freshwater dolphins surviving in these rivers, but they are expected to be extinct in a hundred years. The Yangtze alligators will be extinct in a few years.

Before 1960, the Aral Sea, in central Asia between Kazakhstan and Uzbekistan, was once the fourth largest inland sea, slightly smaller than Lake Superior. When two feeder rivers were diverted to irrigate rice paddies and cotton fields, it began to shrink. Now this sea is half its previous area and has lost three-fourth of its volume. Only one fish survives, the mudfish. What are its needs? Create a story from a water animal's point of view of how it feels trying to survive in a disappearing lake. The unique *tugay* forests that covered 13,000 square kilometers around the lake have shrunk to only 1,000 square kilometers. Can you represent the kilometers in a graph, or can you find cities that represent both numbers? In 1960, there were 173 species of mammals. In 2003, there were only 38 species, and the groups of rhinos and hippopotamuses have reduced drastically. Do research and find out what the extinct species were like. Migrant and nesting birds have fallen from 500 to 285 species. Of course, all regional plants have also dwindled.

Lake Chad is in the center of Africa on the edge of the Sahara Desert. Before 1960, it was a lush, vibrant watering hole for millions of animals. It is flat and shallow, about seven meters deep, so when the water began to dry up, the lake shrank quickly.

Once the sixth largest lake in the world covering 25,000 square kilometers, Lake Chad now covers only one-tenth of its former area. Find out how many square kilometers it covers now and how much has been lost. Rainfall is a significant factor behind this phenomenon, but basically, humans are responsible. During a high-water period in the early sixties, the Southern Chad Irrigation Project was started in Nigeria. Nigeria is one of the four countries surrounding Lake Chad. Find out what the others are. The SCIP began a system of pumps and canals supplying water to farmland. The plan was to resettle 55,000 farming families in this area. As the water decreased, the plan failed. The canals were not lined with plastic, and vast amounts of water soaked into the ground before it got to the farms.

Unfortunately, the 2002 World Summit on Sustainable Development did not discuss water issues. One National Wildlife Federation scientist expressed his concern: "We have no real choices here. Either we as a species live within the limits of the water cycle and utilize it rationally, or we could end up in constant competition with each other and with nature over remaining supplies. Ultimately, if nature loses, we lose." It is estimated that $5 trillion a year is needed to stabilize water systems on our earth. Without this investment, the ecosystems of plants and animals that humans depend on will end up in nightmarish scenarios.

# CHAPTER 4

# UNITED STATES ISSUES

*We are witnessing something unprecedented:*
*Water no longer flows downhill.*
*It flows toward money.*

—Robert Kennedy

*Water is the only drink for a wise man.*

—Henry David Thoreau

The water we drink across the United States has traces of ibuprofen, antibiotics, and fifty-six other pharmaceuticals.

According to a 2007 U.S. Natural Resources Defense Council, at least thirty-six states will face water shortage before 2012. Stabilizing water sources is expected to cost $300 billion over the next thirty years. In 2000, the United States used 148 trillion gallons of water, which amounts to 5 million gallons for each person. Make an illustration that represents these numbers. It is predicted that by 2050, the U.S. population will increase by over 100 million people, and the world will have 9 billion. What will that mean for water issues?

Florida and California face the problem of fast-growing populations, as well as that of saltwater seeping into their underground freshwater. Colorado's population increased by 31% from 1990 to 2000. Nevada's population rose 66% in that period. Nationally, suburban sprawl causes the loss of two acres of farmland every minute. The runoff from parking lots and roads is directed to rivers rather than to replenishing the water table.

California's wildfires, caused by drought, are destroying expensive mountain homes. Recently, there was a major drought in Georgia. The pavement runoff alone could meet the needs of over 3 million people each year. Georgia allowed irrigation on cotton farms. They also allowed a theme park to build a million-gallon mountain of artificial snow. Atlanta's urban sprawl continues. Having little rain is a natural phenomenon that has been made worse by human decisions. Florida and Alabama are fighting against Atlanta's water use.

The rivers of West Virginia and Kentucky are heavy with coal slurry and wastewater from the country's fourth largest coal producer, Massey Energy. The company has been fined $20 million and has pledged to invest millions for pollution control at its forty-four sites.

In the Los Angeles region, lead, mercury, and other pollutants are discharged from factory smokestacks. The foul air contacts rivers and lakes, polluting the waters. Fresno County, California, uses more water than any county in the United States. Farms in its central valley grow many kinds of fruits and vegetables.

Upstate New York reservoirs are at record lows.

The Idaho Department of Water Resources has had to intervene between the farmers pumping water for irrigation and those pumping water to the east Snake River aquifer that stores water for the cities.

The Sierra Nevada snowpack is melting faster each year.

The level of the Great Lakes is falling and is expected to continue doing so because of global warming. This means more dredging to keep shipping lanes open. Antipollution agreements are being negotiated between the Great Lakes states to protect water quality. In 2007, the Great Lakes Water Resources Compact was approved by all adjoining states.

Water Science for Schools (http://ga.water.usgs.gov/edu/) is a huge site with activities in over fifty languages. There are charts to keep track of a home's water use for a week. There is an interdisciplinary group activity that uses buckets of water. If you have Internet access, log on now. If you don't have access, skip to the next section. Pick a topic and prepare a poster board to present to your class. Can you figure out how much rain falls in your area or in Los Angles? Can you make bar graphs? What other types of comparisons can you make?

Under Water—Science topics—Special topics—Opinion.

How can you present this information? Now go to **Challenge Question # 1**: "How much water does it take to grow a hamburger?" Do it yourself, and then ask four other people to do it. (Wonder how your mom or dad would score.) Compare the answers for presentation on your chart. Now go to the source—International Bottled Water Association—and discover more information. Take the Groundwater Quiz, and note in your journal how you did. Then try the dripping-faucet question. Visit the **Questionnaires** page and make more notes in your journal. Finally, check out the information in the Galleries. There are maps, pictures, and databases. Journal and plan your expanding poster.

In the United States, the largest percentage of water is used to make electricity. Does that make sense to you? Investigate how water is used in power plants. The second largest use, at 34%, is irrigation. It takes 16 gallons of water to make one apple and 65 gallons to make a glass of milk. It takes 1,303 gallons to make a hamburger but only 408 gallons for a serving of chicken. Public use of water is only 11%. North and South Dakota use the least water. What do you think is the reason? Texas, California, and Florida use the most water. They are all on oceans. Does that make a difference? What does?

It's hard to estimate how much water a family uses because one person might be washing dishes and rinsing a lot, while with another, it may be a quicker process. New toilets use less water than old ones.

A bath takes about 50 gallons and a shower 2 gallons per minute. How long could you shower before the water use is the same as that of a bath? A dishwasher takes 20 gallons per load, and washing dishes by hand takes 5 gallons. Washing clothes takes 10 gallons. A toilet flush is between 3-7 gallons. Brushing your teeth and washing your hands or face, each take 1 gallon. Figure out your family's water usage, and compare it with that of another family with the same number of people (http://ga.water.usgs.gov/edu/).

The Institute for Agriculture and Trade Policy (IATP) has a policy paper on ethanol as a replacement for gas. Most ethanol plants are in the Midwest, where corn must often be irrigated. In the process of making ethanol, water is recycled and used to cool the fields. But most plants require 5-6 gallons of water for each gallon of ethanol that is produced (www.ethanolrfa.org). New techniques are using only 3 gallons per gallon, but there has been a 254% increase in the amount of water used from 198 to 2008. In Minnesota in 2008, there were seventeen ethanol plants, with ten more being built. Make a large graph to illustrate the increasing numbers. If your scale is small, you won't understand the significance. In 2000, Minnesota produced 220 million gallons of ethanol. In 2008, 734 million gallons were produced, and 1.8 billion gallons are expected to be produced in 2022. The agribusiness community recommends that the ethanol plants use municipal wastewater instead of potential drinking water. It also recommends that feedlots for cattle be located next to ethanol plants so that the leftover ethanol grain can be used efficiently.

In 1972, a national Clean Water Act was passed. Since then, the supreme court rulings have altered the statute. Wetlands are not subject to the act. Only "relatively permanent standing or flowing bodies of water" are now covered. But wetlands are crucial to the health of ecosystems and to the protection for flooding. Creeks that flow in the spring but dry up in the summer are not covered; thus, companies can pollute the land, and the spring runoff goes into our rivers and lakes.

http://wrc.umn.edu/outreach/index.html

# CHAPTER 5

# ISSUES AROUND THE WORLD

*A new scientific truth is not usually presented in a way to convince its opponents. Rather, they die off, and a rising generation is familiarized with the truth from the start.*

—Max Planck

*To acquire knowledge, one must study; but to acquire wisdom, one must observe.*

—Marilyn von Savant

Each year, 25 million people die from contaminated water. That is equal to the whole population of Canada. There are 1.4 billion people who have difficulty getting clean water. By 2020, it is expected that the world will need 40% more water because of growing populations. The UN predicts that in 2025, about 2.8 billion people in forty-eight countries will be facing water stress.

The news article from April 2006 begins, "Hundreds of machete-wielding farmers opposed to a hydroelectric dam project briefly seized a pumping plant, cutting off much of the water supply to Acapulco just days before tourists flock to the Pacific resort for their Easter vacations." The protesters ended a two-week blockade that wanted to teach the people of Acapulco what a water shortage was like. The protesters believe the day will dry up their farms and fisheries.

In 2007, southern Europe experienced extremely hot temperatures, with rainfall short by 50%. In 2007, The Canary Islands, which is normally a mild climate, experienced day temperatures that rose as high as 104 degrees.

South America uses 26% of the earth's water with only 6% of the world's population. North America uses 8% with only 15%. Europe has 13% and only uses 8% water. Asia has 60% of the world's population and uses only 36% of the water. People in Kenya use about 3 gallons of water a day while people in the UK use 30 gallons and the Unites States/Canada use 150 gallons a day. In India, 70% of the lakes and rivers are unsafe for drinking or bathing. Ninety percent of China's groundwater is contaminated. By 2050, the world's population is expected to be almost 2.9 billion, with 90% growth in the poverty-bound areas of developing countries.

In India, Coca-Cola and Pepsi have pumped so much water to make their soft drinks that the water table has lowered drastically, forcing local people to get their water from polluted streams. The water Coke uses in one day is enough to meet the needs of twenty thousand Indians. In addition, the waste liquid from the plants is so polluted that it can't be used to irrigate rice paddies. India did not have laws regulating the tapping of groundwater. More than twenty U.S. universities have banned Coca-Cola products on their campuses in protest against the human rights abuses.

The World Bank estimates that 21% of the communicable diseases in India are caused by unsafe drinking water. If eight two-hundred-passenger jets crashed, the public's attention would be riveted. Preventable diarrhea kills more than that many Indian people each and every day. Only 14% of the rural population use latrines. Hand washing in these areas is infrequent. On the other hand, are you aware that Indians are fast becoming our computer technicians, answering our distress calls over phone when our computers malfunction? They are also trained to have the English accent according to the region of the United States they are serving so they sound like a New Yorker or a Southwesterner when they speak. Farmers and city dwellers pump their water out from rapidly declining water tables with tube wells. Yet the Indian government has not made adequate plans for meeting the needs of the rapidly growing population.

Neighboring Bangladesh, once part of India, also has major water problems. It is a low-lying country, about the size of New York State. It is one of the poorest countries in the world, packed with over 140 million people. Major areas flood with the monsoon rains each year. Arsenic is common in one-fourth of the Bangladesh wells. It causes vomiting, stomach pain, hard patches on the skin, and many types of cancer. In one area, 60% of the wells are painted red to indicate that they contain arsenic. Two-year-old children can have arsenicosis. Arsenic filtration systems are at work, but they lose effectiveness over time. People are being taught to collect rainwater during the rainy season, but they do not have storage systems to keep it for the dry season. The research in Bangladesh has helped identify arsenic poisoning in India and China. Half of the Bangladeshi people live in poverty. Every year, 110,000 children under five years die from water-related diseases. More than twenty international organizations are working to provide safe water and education on hygiene.

Another issue is the Bangla rivers that flow in from India. As India uses up the river water, or pollutes it, the water quality and quantity in Bangladesh is immediately affected.

When I visited Dhaka, the Bangladesh capital, I saw little children begging in the streets all through the day and far into the night. In the slums, water vendors make illegal taps in the city's water supply and sell water to the slum residents. Can you imagine living in a cardboard box and having to buy water? Write in your journal about these children living in Dhaka's slums. How would you feel begging for water for hours each day and getting only enough to survive but not to wash? Recently, WaterAid and its partner DSK have set up water pickup stations. Could you create a money-raising event to help educate other students and their families? Encourage them to make a contribution to WaterAid America at 212-683-0430.

Can you imagine urine running down the streets? I've seen it in Dhaka. School children play a big role in helping families learn better ways of sanitation because teachers spend a lot of time explaining better health habits. I went to Bangladesh for UNICEF to train teachers how to be more engaging and thus help students stay in school. Bangladesh's goal is to have all children finish the fifth grade. Things are improving in Bangladesh, but the problem is so large it will take quite a while.

In central Asia, the Aral Sea was once the fourth largest lake. Now it has lost 80% of its water, causing sixty-thousand fishing jobs to disappear. Its two feeding rivers have been diverted to irrigate cotton. The dry lake bed is poisoned by pesticides, and the remaining water is too saline to be used. By 2015, it is expected to be completely dry.

In Iran, the water table has been falling by 2.8 meters a year. How does that compare with the height of the tallest student in your class? "Water refugees" are leaving areas where wells are dry.

Saudi Arabia's wheat crop dropped by 34% in fifteen years. And neighboring Yemen's water table is dropping at the rate of six meters a year. Figure out how high your classrooms' ceiling is and compare.

Only 22% of Ethiopia's people have safe water, and only 13% have adequate bathroom facilities. It is worse in the rural areas, where the choice is for women and children to walk up to six hours for water, carrying water jugs weighing up to forty pounds. Many people choose to collect water from the shallow ponds that the animals use. In the last twenty years, Ethiopia has had repeated droughts, causing depletion in food supplies. Diarrhea, pneumonia, measles, malaria, and tuberculosis are common, in addition to malnutrition. That explains why the median age in this country is only eighteen years. Write a paragraph in your journal about what you assume would be the doctor and hospital situation in such a scenario. One hundred miles south of the capital city is the Lake Ziway region. Here, with international help, people have learned how to create irrigation ditches that facilitate the planting of corn and vegetables. Farmers have been taught soil conservation, fertilizer use, and marketing of their produce.

Kenya is also water poor as a result of droughts, rampant deforestation, unfair water allocation, population explosion, and poor management by government. Write down your ideas on why these poor countries have population explosions. Only 61% of the rural people have safe water, with 43% sanitation. (Sanitation means outhouses, not toilets that use water.) Because women and children spend much of their day walking for water, there is little time for children, especially girls, to go to school. In all countries, women do the water work as part of housekeeping. Most are responsible for their gardens also. On March 20, 2000, a large group of thirsty monkeys attacked villagers when the water truck arrived. During the two-hour melee, eight monkeys were killed and ten villagers were injured. In our effort to give people water, we often overlook the needs of animals. Dying populations of animals change the ecosystem.

In the Rwenzori Mountains, between Uganda and the Republic of Congo, 84% of the glaciers have disappeared. Alpine rivers have dwindled, plants have died, and farming has been impacted by climate change. The indigenous people believe that the reason for the lack of snow is that the young turned away from traditional customs and made the father of spirits, Nzururu, angry. The warmer temperatures have also brought malaria that was never experienced before.

On World Water Day (March 22, 2007), over five thousand people marched down the streets of San Salvador in Central America to protest the "high cost of water, unjust distribution of water, contaminated water and environmental destruction." Next to El Salvador is Guatemala. Here the median age is 18.9 years. Those who live to be adults are mostly illiterate (70.6%), and the same is the case in El Salvador (80.2%) as well. In the poorer region of the Mayan villages, it is hard to find water, but overall, 95% of the people have water and 86% proper sanitation. Honduras, east of Guatemala, has a median age of 19.7 years. In the United States, 60% of our people are between ages twenty and sixty-four. The U.S. poverty rate is 12.6%, while it is 53% in Honduras. Improved sanitation is 69%, and safe water is 87%. Honduras is often hit by hurricanes that eliminate safe water for months until reconstruction. Mosquitoes carry malaria and dengue fever in addition to waterborne diseases like cholera.

Half of the flowers sold in the United States are grown in Columbia, causing water-stress issues. Deforestation in the Andes Mountains is significantly reducing the water supply. Columbia has one of the largest diversity of plants and animals. This beautiful country is losing flora and fauna because of the shortage of water.

Large water corporations have convinced governments that they would do a better job of providing water for communities. In the book *Troubled Waters*, the author reports that privatization of water has significantly increased water prices: 400% in the Philippines, 150% in France with worse water quality, 450% in England, while the salaries of CEOs in companies increased by 708%.

In Bolivia, just west of water-abundant Brazil, people fought the U.S. company Bechtel for buying over the water system from the government. The company, having acquired the water system, had tripled the cost of water. A family earning $100 a month was charged $20 for water. Thousands of people marched in protest, blocking traffic and effectively shutting down the capital city. A month later, they staged a peaceful protest and were attacked by police with tear gas that left 175 people injured and two dead. A survey of sixty thousand people showed that 90% wanted Bechtel gone. The president responded by suspending civil rights and banning any gathering of more than four people. Radio stations were taken over by the military. Newspaper reporters were arrested. The mayor, trained in the School of Americas in Fort Benning, Georgia, knew how to terrorize citizens. (Are we still training terrorists in Georgia today?) Farmers erected roadblocks to major cities, cutting off food supplies. In the cities, angry residents armed with rocks and sticks fought with the police. Finally, Bechtel withdrew! The people's victory in Bolivia stirred the hearts of people in the Philippines, Australia, and Scotland, where the governments had signed contracts with the parent company of Bechtel.

The World Bank was involved in Bolivia and, according to its Web site, is currently active in 582 places. Its mission is to alleviate poverty worldwide. There are diverse water-related problem sites in Ukraine, Armenia, Afghanistan, Guyana, Senegal, and Egypt. In Romania, the World Bank halted a $100-million loan that would create an open-pit gold and silver mine. It would have used cyanide to process the gold. In 2000, a cyanide-tailing dam was split open, polluting the Tisza and Danube rivers, contaminating water for 2.5 million people and killing tons of fish.

Wheat is the most important crop in northern semiarid China. Due to water shortages, the crop has declined by 15% in ten years. Yet China's population is rapidly growing.

http://water.org/waterpartners.aspx?pgID=883
www.bicn.com/acic West Bengal & Bangladesh Arsenic Crisis Information Centre

# CHAPTER 6

# THE GOOD NEWS

*Thousands have lived without love,*
*not one without water.*

—W. H. Auden

*When one tugs at a single thing in nature*
*He finds all is connected.*

—Anonymous

In the highlands of western Ethiopia, communities have maintained their wetlands by protecting springs and native plants and limiting overuse. Their excellent practices have been used for 250 years.

In a remote African village in Kenya, the only water was from a polluted river that the animals used. It was full of harmful germs and had turned so ugly with dirt that visitors would shun it. Then, Procter & Gamble launched their "Children's Safe Drinking Water" (www.csdworg) program that brought in the PUR water purifier. The villagers now fill a bucket and stir in the water treatment packet. In twenty minutes, the water begins to clear and is safe to drink.

In Kathmandu, the United Nations Habitat for Asian Cities Program of the 1980s has produced excellent results. It created model houses that collect, clean, and store rainwater. The people use wastewater from the kitchen and from washing for their gardens. People are also taught to use earthworms to process household waste. "Dry toilets" have been created to process both urine and bowel movements into reusable fertilizer for flowers. In the United States, a toilet flush used 3.5 gallons, but now there is a "dual flush" toilet, which uses only 0.6 gallon when there is just urine.

In Japan, water from the sink is routed to the toilet's water tank.

A Swiss company, LifeStraw, has created a 1 × 10 inch plastic tube with an activated charcoal interior that filters parasites and bacteria from contaminated water. It costs a few dollars, and charitable groups are distributing them. KickStart, a San Francisco company, sells a $35 leg-powered water pump for farming.

Another Swiss company, SODIS (solar water disinfection), puts unsafe water into recycled plastic bottles and then sets them on a corrugated metal sheet in the sun for a few hours. Children using this water are seven times less likely to get cholera and have a 20% lower chance of diarrhea.

WaterPartners has worked all over the world, providing grants and expertise for water management. It has now created the WaterCredit Initiative designed to help grassroots communities to play a bigger role in determining how to handle their needs.

PlayPumps International, a nonprofit organization, has brought thousands of merry-go-rounds into sub-Saharan Africa. The system attaches a merry-go-round to a pump and storage tank that taps well water. As the children play, the water is pumped.

The University of Minnesota's Water Resources Center does research on water-related problems and reaches out to better educate the public. One group of researchers studies the benefits of using processed liquid manure to fertilize corn. Other studies deal with feedlot management where cattle are fattened up before slaughter.

The Water Resources Center has launched environmental restoration projects relating to the drainage of marshes, and it sends *The Shoreland* newsletter to over seven hundred shore-land property owners.

The Nutrients and Water Quality section of the center studies aquatic ecosystems and trains farmers to create plans for fertilizing practices that protect groundwater and streams. There is also a volunteer stream-monitoring partnership that trains individuals to gather information on lakes and rivers and sends it to the university for analysis and feedback. Friends of the Mississippi is one of the participants in this enterprise. There are over two thousand volunteers monitoring sixty sites.

The University of Minnesota Water Resource Center also monitors drinking water, manages watershed issues, and provides speakers for schools.

Individual homeowners can be guided by the Greywater Guerrillas to recycle water from their showers, sinks, and washers into water for their gardens. To find out more, go to the Web site watersavertech.com. Here you can find more information about a system that funnels your sink water to the toilet, thus reusing the water.

Another company from the UK, Rainharvesting Systems LTD., advertises that their system of pipes and storage tanks can provide water for laundry and gardening. See their Web site.

A Minnesota company, Pentair, has partnered with WaterHealth to form a new Indian company, which has 575 employees working in eighty sites. The water systems are built in Goa, delivered, and pipes are connected to unsafe water supplies. Workers perform water tests every day, maintain water quality, and distribute the water in twenty-liter jugs. Get five-liter bottles and figure out how many gallons is equal to this. Then try walking some miles, or at least around your school, carrying the filled 5-liter bottles. Write in your journal about your experience. The general manager of Pentair once spoke about his early days in India when people fought to get in line as they believed the safe water would run out. Now it is orderly, with people taking off their shoes as if they are entering a temple. He spoke of a woman who was sick and had gotten healthy. She created a booklet to share with others and walked barefoot from house to house to explain where to get the safe water. "Our goal," he explains, "is to install systems in 50 villages a month." It costs about $5,000 to install a system. Make some notes in your journal about this project, and figure out how much it costs a month. Pentair Water India now has a research center in New Delhi with a hundred scientists working on better ways to collect rainwater and device smaller, more efficient systems.

An article from England begins with "Ken Livingstone caused a bit of a stink this summer by encouraging Londoners not to rush to flush." Water companies are offering water meters to families and encouraging them to save water. Saving water saves money for families. Manufacturing companies that save significant amounts are presented the Water Efficiency Award and publicly praised.

A new company in Great Britain, Belu, has developed a biodegradable water bottle made from cornmeal. It takes only twelve weeks to decompose, and all profits go to clean-water projects around the world. Their first project was concerned with wells and hand pumps in an Indian village providing safe water for ten thousand people in the area. They are working in Mali in partnership with WaterAid. An additional project is cleaning debris from the Thames River.

Improved irrigation systems are available in drip and other microirrigation methods that can significantly reduce the water consumption as well as increase crop production. More than two hundred thousand farmers worldwide, including 30% of India's farmers, are using these technologies.

It has been proven that high-quality rice can be grown while letting fields dry between irrigations. This has the potential of reducing water needs from 10% to 70%, thereby freeing water for other uses. Madagascar's poor soil is now waving 50% of the water with a significant increase in rice yields.

Around Lake Nakuru in Kenya, forests were cut down to provide farmland for a growing population. As the trees disappeared, the rain decreased and the lake began to shrink. In addition, chemical runoff from the farms polluted what was left of the lake, killing fish and birds. The lake had a large population of flamingos that attracted tourists. As the flamingos disappeared, so did the tourists; this had a major impact on the economy of these already poor people. The community realized they needed the trees more than the farmland. In 2007, people planted more than three thousand trees. Now the lake is healing, and the flamingos have returned.

People in North America are becoming more aware of the amount of water it takes to meat. If people could reduce their meat consumption by half, the water used would be reduced by 37%. For ten grams of protein in eggs, it takes 244 liters of water. For ten grams of beef, it takes 1,000 liters. Use these figures in a graph.

# CONCLUSION

Water is vital to all forms of life. The United States has repeatedly failed to create enough funding for water issues. Cities and states are dealing with local issues, but we have no national program. We need a federal trust fund for clean water. You may find out more at www.foodandwaterwatch.org/water/trust-fund. As students, you can help to educate others. Give speeches in your community and church. Talk to relatives and friends. Write articles for your newspapers. The power is yours. The problem is yours. Your learning mind will lead the way!